W9-CYZ-643

TRILOGY OF DANCE

Passion of the Dance
Power of the Dance
Pleasure of the Dance

Janice Sussman

trimark press

LIBRARY OF CONGRESS CATALOGING-IN-PUBLICATION DATA

TRILOGY OF DANCE

JANICE SUSSMAN

P. CM.
ISBN: 978-1-943401-13-0 · HARDCOVER EDITION
ISBN: 978-1-943401-05-5 · SOFTCOVER EDITION
LIBRARY OF CONGRESS CONTROL NUMBER: 2015951848

J15
10 9 8 7 6 5 4 3 2 1
FIRST EDITION
PRINTED AND BOUND IN THE UNITED STATES OF AMERICA

WWW.TRILOGYOFDANCE.COM

368 SOUTH MILITARY TRAIL
DEERFIELD BEACH, FL 33442
800.889.0693
WWW.TRIMARKPRESS.COM

To my wonderful husband who is the spine of my existence. He has given me the courage to take the magic of belief and make it real.

"There is only one of you in all time. This expression is unique, and if you block it, it will never exist through any other medium and be lost."

—Martha Graham

TRILOGY OF DANCE

THE KISS

Can you see the Pleasure of the Dance?
Can you feel it in the deconstructed
Parts of the kiss?
Can you imagine the peak of its
Existence?

Come with me inside the embrace.
Kiss me to pleasure
And we will dance

On the Cover: THE KISS by Neil Grayson

Neil Grayson's THE KISS embraces the spirit of dance explored in Janice Sussman's *Trilogy of Dance.* His painting captivates with its power. We feel the strength of position, the dynamic of connection. It is here where art and dance join in the timelessness of perfection and lead us to pleasure. The painting breathes, it lives, it finds meaning in the energy of the universe as two souls become one.

"Find the courage to express the You that is You. Bathe it in truth. Dance it with Joy. Savor the moment."

—Janice Sussman

CONTENTS

Dancers, judges, coaches, performers,
and organizers share their innermost
thoughts and tell us... *Why We Dance.*

PREFACE

Janice Sussman has written three poetry collections about ballroom dance, and in this one volume, you have them all in your hand. Her journey into ballroom dance has been transformative. The paradox of any art form is that the more deeply the artist surrenders to the rules of the craft, the more powerfully the artist comes to control the outward form of the work. Through these poems, you will follow Janice's journey from novice to expert dancer. At first, she is overwhelmed but attentive, but over time she masters the rules, and in the end she can find the spaces of calm within the frenzy. Her attraction may have started in her desire to escape into a fantasy, but what Janice learns on the dance floor ultimately became a part of her day-to-day reality. The escape became a home, and being at home on the dance floor has made her more at home in her own life, in her own (as they say) skin.

The first two parts of this collection were previously published as chapbooks under the name Alessandra West. Alessandra wasn't merely a pseudonym; she was an alter ego, with her own biography and her own personality. Like Eve being plucked from Adam, Alessandra was pulled from Janice. On the surface, Alessandra was made of the sexiest, smoothest, youngest parts of Janice, but to the more careful reader, the undercurrents of Alessandra were made of Janice's most vulnerable and inexperienced parts. Alessandra had never started a non-profit, the way Janice has, never raised children the way Janice has, never loved grandchildren the way Janice has. I am going to miss Alessandra, but I'd like to think that having been called into being, and having served Janice well, she can now return to the ether, like Ariel at the end of the *Tempest*. I may also be getting sentimental—after all, Alessandra is still here in the book.

Many of Janice's readers have come to her through the world of dance, and they are intimately acquainted with the experiences that Janice/Alessandra explore in this collection. Many of them will have personally joined Janice on her journey. I, however, have been on a different journey with Janice. We have been exploring poetry together for the better part of a decade, and I am thrilled to see Janice's progress as a poet. Poetry is often compared to song, but poetry is also very close to dance. People often forget that poetry is a physical, bodily experience. I am not surprised that for Janice, dance and poetry have been parallel art forms in which to apprentice, grow, and excel. You hold in your hands the fruit of Janice's love for two arts. My advice: get comfortable and enjoy!

Jason Schneiderman
Brooklyn, 2015

INTRODUCTION

In the prelude to her book *The Dance,* Oriah invites her reader with these beautiful words: "Take me to the places on the earth that teach you how to dance, the places where you can risk letting the world break your heart, and I will take you to the places where the earth beneath my feet and the stars overhead make my heart whole again and again."

Alessandra West has been travelling the same journey as Oriah, rushing to share each step of orgasmic frenzy in the dance. In *Passion of the Dance* and *Power of the Dance,* Alessandra brings you the tactile sensations of dance.

Now the touch and the music and the passion have given her the confidence to dance at the sunrise of a new existence. Her rebirth happened in the quiet of morning as time stood still. There was darkness to transcend, fear to overcome. Courageously she faced the light. Leaving fantasy behind, writing under her own name for the first time, shedding Alessandra, grasping reality, she finds the pleasure on the dance floor of life and says, "I am I."

And so the story begins anew. I still remember the very first time. I said shyly, "Let's talk a bit." He shook his head and replied, "No, let's dance." Gently he took my hand and looked into my eyes and lit the flame that carried me to the point of no return. There was no return as I walked hesitantly into a cave of my unexplored emotions. Yes, I took the first step, and yes, he led the way.

The strains of the Rumba had me moving, even though I didn't know how or where. I just wanted to feel the music and his touch. He was kind, and he touched my goodness. I dreamed the dream and began dancing my dance with passion. I let it flow to wherever it led me, to wherever my thoughts took me, to wherever I captured the taste and feel on the page so I could let you share the how and why.

It took a year or maybe even two to reach my first climax—to get to the pinnacle and look down at the world happening on the dance floor. And so *Power of the Dance* was created by the tension of touch and the strength of my desire to give birth to myself, to let the power flow, to surrender to the power of expression, the power given to me through the dance.

Now, here I am, ready to stand before you in *Pleasure of the Dance*. I have taken on a new form and deeper awareness. I have looked in the mirror and seen myself reborn. I reach out for this journey to my new partner, Craig Gordon. I reach out to him with trust. I reach out to him in truth. The richness of our dance fills me with joy. Dance causes time to lose its control. Dance allows me to feel, to be, to become my own spirit. I am complete when I dance. It is why I dance. It is *Why We Dance!*

Janice Sussman
Boca Raton, 2015

TRILOGY OF DANCE

PASSION OF
THE DANCE
(2011)

I am the alter ego of every woman who asks, WHO AM I?
Trapped by the good girl. Shackled by the shoulds.
Unleashed by the passion of the dance.

Give me your eyes. Give me your ears. Give me your soul.
And I will give you the courage to admit that you, too,
share this longing. You will feel its power, dance its dance
and cry out in release as it sets you free.

—Alessandra West

THE NEXT STEP

"We're going to the next step," he said
And looked me straight in the eye for the first time
Honestly holding me firmer so I could feel the him
Of him rolling around my middle and honestly
It felt good and even though I should have been
Looking and feeling and waiting for the visual lead
I was lost again in my own world of imagining the
Pleasure of an intimacy promised by the words of
The song and the movement of his body and the
Urge I felt to stop pretending I was pretending
And wanted to feel it all roughly and deliciously and
Strongly and brilliantly... so I could be led.

THE LESSON

His hand pushed my hip to a rise.
Our legs touched along their lengths
As I began to feel the heat causing
Sweat to form at the nape of my neck.

It'll come easier once you read
The signal of my lead. You'll feel it
With my hand on your back or the
Roll of my body on your thigh.

Look into my eyes. It's more than
The feet that matter. Give me room
From the waist down to show them
All I can do to make you look good.

But by then his words were lost in the music
And the power of his touch and the warmth
Of his breath as magic took over roaming
With us on a wooden floor that was melting.

WORTH PRETENDING

When he picked up his shirt to
Show me a raised hip I knew
I was in trouble because I was
Looking at skin, the smoothness
Of skin, the color of skin, the
Texture of skin, his skin tempting

Me. It was all I could do to keep my
Hands to myself even though
One hand was placed properly
Holding his with just enough
Pressure to make sure I knew
Where I was going.

It was the other hand that wanted
To be naughty, that was pretending
It didn't know what to do but
Really had done it before. Then
He showed me how to place
It suggestively but I was

Well beyond suggestion. We kept
The sex at bay but let it play with
Our minds, letting desire lurk behind
The heat of our bodies fueled by knowing
Nothing would happen but tempting each
Other to the point of breathlessness.

SUCH IS THE SAMBA

Over and over again I reach for my head.
No, no, stop the volta right here before you
Lead me uncontrollably into a roll where
My feet lose contact with the floor but
Not with the length of your body.

Over and over again I'll keep my hip high
With heels raised and legs straight
Making it difficult to end in the corner
But easy enough to turn twice before
Stopping with arm raised and pointing.

Over and over again I end facing you
Touching your chest roughly with
My palm pushing away from you
Allowing me to continue in a path

Heated by the samba beat, sexy
Hot, angry, firm, oozing, wet, wild.

RUMBA WALK

Today we practiced a rumba walk
For two hours of pushing hips in
Rhythm to a beat that would lead
Nowhere but to the edge of the
Bed where you would tickle more
Than my fancy to stop the gnawing
Desire I have to grab and squeeze and get
To a part that is so deep it hurts to be
There but wants it in anticipation of
More than hurt, yes, pleasure of a rare
Kind that will sear your skin into broiling.

I KEEP TRYING

You keep wanting my head to be at
Five eleven and I keep trying but
It wants to be somewhere else like
In the curve of your arm or on your
Chest because then I feel warm not
Stand-off-ish cold taking a disciplined
Shape on the dance floor conforming
To tradition, being judged for the
Exactness of the step not allowing
Me to be the self that I need to be.

Hip to hip doesn't do it like body to
Body, neck to neck, hand to skin
Searching for a oneness that tries to
Come close on the dance floor but doesn't
Make it like when you grab me twelve
To six or six to nine or seven to seven
On the floor next to the fireplace where
The warmth of the flames match the warmth
Of our bodies making the longing disappear.

Dancing is the tease in real time giving
A hint of what could be but asking us to
Keep it confined to the boundaries of the
Ballroom, some longer and narrow, some wider
Some square but trying to be round like the circle
Of life or you breathing life into my ear
Touching my hair, smelling my smell and
Asking me to dip gracefully, spin with control
Move toward center with a one, two, three
Yet rise in time to catch the beat of your heart.

THEY PRACTICED

They practiced in simple black clothing
Outlining their strict, tall bodies.
Their legs appeared endless as they
Crossed the room gracefully in two
Large turns repeating the moves
Over and over again in rhythm
With their heartbeats, sometimes
Exchanging words of encouragement
And sometimes harshness.

I couldn't take my eyes off them
Because they were living the
Yearning I had inside to be better
Than I am, to win, to practice, to
Prepare for the performance, to

Take life by the hand and lead it,
Not taking for granted the work
It takes to make perfection look easy
To be ready for the applause.

They were a young couple in
Age but in experience, showing
Me they had learned life lessons
On the dance floor as he placed
His hand on her back encouraging
Her to lean into his strength yet
Demanding that she hug the floor
With both feet using her toes for
Balance as she responded to his touch.

They skated across the practice floor
On beams of fading afternoon sunshine
Never breaking the hip to hip position
Bending as one, as if a gentle breeze
Accompanied the music of the dance.
And yet in one brief moment reality crept
Into an intimate corner of the room as they
Playfully grasped fingers, making me smile.

DON'T MAKE ME STOP

I don't want to stop dancing
Because sometimes when I do I
Start crying like it happened
Today after dancing and stopping
And sitting looking out over the Bay
With glassy eyes dreaming of
What might have been or what
Could be and knowing it is
All the fantasy that happens
On the Ballroom Floor.

Don't make me stop dancing and
Realize it can't be, because when you
Hold me on the dance floor I
Think it still can and the tears
Now that I have stopped for the
Day are salty and bitter and sad

Like the ending of the day with the
Sun vanishing on the skyline
Leaving me as if I didn't happen at all.

Let me continue to believe I can
Make your skin tingle with my touch
As our legs become one agreeing to
Move forward to a beat we are making
Come alive with the energy of our
Souls responding to the rhythm of
The song or the call of the words.
Let's not take it nice and easy but
Fly away with Frank or Johnny or
Barbra clinging to the perfection of a waltz

RUMBA POWER ON TUESDAY

I walked onto the dance floor that Tuesday
Already ready because "Sway With Me" was
Playing and had me imagining his heat as he
Came toward me reaching for my hand.

In the blackness of his eyes I could tell he, too,
Was ready as he pulled me in roughly till I
Faced him with bent legs angled just enough
To fit between his and feel the pressure of his hips.

It was the start of a routine where the next move
Had my hands groping for connection, fingers spread wide
Along his thigh before they led the way to his knees, before
He reached for me, before I reached back showing my willingness

To play with death, to take a chance that his offer was
Real and would find relief in the tightness of my grasp
As we breathed the beat letting the power explode in the
Climax of the movement making us shudder to the count, four and...

THE HEAT OF ARGENTINE TANGO

It hung on the wall, more than a painting
A battle of the sexes, a couple wrapped
Onto each other in a step common to
The Argentine Tango but uncommon
To those needing space or time or distance

They had found perfect expression for
Their passion in a hold that takes strength
And a desire to give into the music and
Let the heat carry them to a different place
Where temptation wins and lust triumphs

Fitted perfectly in a frame yet waiting to be
Released from constraint, with legs pressing forward
In anger, back in refusal and together in submission
They danced the Argentine Tango with him in the
Lead, her head buried deep in his chest saying yes

To his nod for all the evening promised.
She wore almost nothing of a red dress yet it
Showed everything on the steamy dance floor
Where imagination turned to reality as we saw
The passion of the dance through the artist's skill.

REHEARSING

They'll never believe I don't drink
Because he kept pouring
And I kept emptying

Like the night you filled the tub
And we jumped in
To cleanliness
Not quite next to godliness
As you rubbed my shoulders
With your knees
And splashed bubbles
Into the air

They'll never believe I don't drink
Because the fake laugh
Appears like it's been rehearsed
For hours
Like the times we spend wrapped
Together rehearsing

Love

PASSION OF THE DANCE

I want the dancer's walk—that twist of hips
Inviting me to do more than follow
I want the thrill as he moistens his lips
Asking me if love is there to borrow
I'm in a new world with music playing
His closeness driving me insane with yearning
He bends his knees and mine while swaying
By dance's end I'm lost in all this turning
I want my hands to flow and feel and sin
To capture all the lust and keep it close
To realize it will happen soon as we begin
To let myself be led by it the most

My innocence is gone, I can't retreat
I live the passion of the dance to feel its heat

RUMBA VS. PASO DOBLE

One, two, three, four and one-close at the knee.
I'll guide you by the wrist. Push, pull and play.
It's temptation and pure sex. Do you see
The "Look of Love" sounds sensuous today.

Do it slowly at first. Legs straight. Don't bend.
Keep them apart most of the time. Not closed.
You play with sex. Know the message you send.
Point. Wink. Lead him on. Propose

Rumba through the night till calves ache.
Twist with delight, shoulders flowing, breasts jab.
Point and slide a little. Don't leave the floor.
Watch your side. Now your waist. He'll grab

You for the Paso Doble. Hate not love.
Sex of a different kind. Attack each move.

WILL YOU DANCE WITH ME?

Will you dance with me till I find
     stillness in the grasp
     of your gentle hands

Will you dance with me till the
     strength of your lead stops
     me once again from falling

Sway with me, touch me
     breathe softly into my hair
     awaken smothered feelings

Tell me it's okay to respond to
     the power of a dip,
     the curve of a sashay

Let me know...

If the end of the dance means it all stops
If the corners of the floor really end in a point

Please, I pray...
Make the reflection go on forever
The refraction become real

Please, I pray...
Dance with me till endless tomorrows
Wipe tears from my crying soul

COME TO US

Take us, hold us, cover
Us with love as we watch
The ocean together. Three
Sets of eyes peering from

Souls yearning to be touched
By hands warm with desire
Telling us we are real and not
Just breasts and legs and openings

Waiting to be filled as you desire
Losing sight of our movement as
The ocean rises and falls in rhythm
That we will match if you let us

For we are strong enough to make
You quiver and fall yet weak enough
To need your closeness. Come to us
Quickly. Before the tide rushes out.

HE DANCES WITH GOD

There is an energy of the dance
That can be felt the minute
The music starts and he asked
Me to feel it before I even moved

My feet and he closed his eyes
And was transformed to a place
That seemed wonderful by the smile
On his lips parted just enough to sigh.

The movement came through his gentle
Hands and undulating body that captured
The light of his spirit and he wanted me to
Be selfish and keep my own light yet join

Him there and I wanted to so badly I ached
To move with his rhythm and not make a
Mistake and show him I trusted his lead
And show him I cared so deeply.

We did basic rumba and basic cha cha but
With him nothing is basic yet everything is
So basic that it penetrates to the core of the
Soul, the place where he dances with God.

HER CHARIOT

Here she comes
Getting out of her
Pumpkin chariot
A little bit nervous
That the Ball has
Already begun and
She'll miss the best
Part of life as the
Dancing begins and
He places her in what
Should be the comfort
Of his arms but turns
Out to be a net where
He throws her back
And forth to the time
Of the music but not
To her rhythm as he
Takes the lead again
And she must follow.

Her gown of brilliant
Red drops from a neckline
That plunges to her
Breasts showing mounds
That want love and
Loving perched with

Longing to be on time
With the rest of her body
And fill the gap between
Her hip and his as they
Rise and fall to the beat
Of the Waltz that looks
Beautiful from outside
But hides the reality of
Her bent knees trying
To hold her up stoically
But seeming to bend in
Half with a helplessness
Only the follower can fake

She wants to be Cinderella
After the clock strikes twelve
When she can dance as her
Heart desires with abandon
And the right to make her
Own line of dance on a floor
Reflecting truth and wisdom
And is smooth enough to let
Her break free from the net
And Dance under the spell of
A silver Moon

THE BEST OF RHYTHM

Time and feeling are one in the space
Of a ballroom floor as their bodies
Catch the rhythm of a Latin pace
And move sensually. He grabs with ease

The nape of her neck, the side of her thigh.
She reaches for him, with craving eyes
And arms sending a message of inviting
Closer touch and a lover's cry.

They play gracefully in rumba rhythm
With pauses that go on forever
Leaving us breathless and squirming
Wanting desire to rise whenever

The time and feeling move us to dance
In the best of rhythm, if we take the chance

TOGETHER

He waltzed me onto the dance floor.
You would think it a perfect dance
Slowly fitting into each other's arms
Waiting for him to take the lead.
But the illusion stops there.

It's not really a show of his strength. It's
Not business as usual. "Hold up your frame.
Keep your arms strong. Use those legs."
Those are the demands of the dance.

Now I must play by different rules
Take my own part on the floor
Stand on my own so the floor doesn't shrink.
No. Stand on my own, so I don't shrink.

And we can dance together so I'm not leaning
Or heavy but light and capable and strong
Accepting the differences. Learning the secret.
Finding out two can be one, still needing the other

PLAYING WITH TEMPTATION

"Let's play," he said. And she turned in disbelief.
Playing was not his style, taking life seriously,
Being so responsible it hurt to be by his side
Captured in the strength with nowhere to go.

And now he seemed to get it, on the tip of his tongue
Brushing smoothly over her ear lobe wanting to go in
And reach for a response too hidden by messages of
Rules and self-doubt and being the "good" girl.

It all started to happen when he relished being rubbed
And found her captured by the taste of his youth.
It all seemed possible now that playing with temptation

Became a regular activity and liking it happened more often.

Now the thrill of possibility took its turn in the list of choices
Arriving first as he came firmly to her side and lifted
Her arm and felt the roundness of her breasts and the hardness
Of her nipples telling him the answer to temptation was, "Yes."

HOW WILL I KNOW?

My heart skipping a beat to the
Quickstep? Dipping to the Waltz?
Was there meaning in his glance?

How will I ever know since dancing
Is about following and not leading?
Answering and not asking?

There's a warmth to his touch as
A spin sets me reeling with dizziness
Trying to catch up with a racing mind

Trying to make sense out of a leading
Hand that sets the tone sparkling
Along with the bubbles he pours

Along with the dream that it begins
At the knees and leads to a promenade
Into the darkness of a smothering night

TOUCH ME MAN TO WOMAN

HE   Touch me like you mean it

SHE   He said as I rumba walked
                 Past him and felt the tightness
                 Of his body melt into my hand

HE   Look me in the eyes. It's me
                 You want more than breath

SHE   And I gasped doing a side step,
                 Bending the passing leg so
                 It would touch teasingly

HE   Place your hand firmly on
                 My back and press deeply

SHE   There's a tenseness between
                 The blades. I know it's from
                 Training to get ready for this

HE   Show me the power of your
                 Step and enough hip to arouse

SHE   I want to do more with these hips
                 Resting them where they belong

HE	I have a need to run my fingers
	Through your hair and curl it
SHE	Touch my hair and you
	Have me all the way
HE	Your breasts are flirtingly rising
	To a fullness I can feel
SHE	I want to feel the softness of
	My skin through the touches of lace
HE	You are wrapping your leg around
	My body knowing I long for it
SHE	Now I feel the rise of him from the
	Toes like the flames of a campfire
HE	The desire reaching my thighs
	Makes me grab harder for real
SHE	I must stop these thoughts and come
	Back to the room of walls and mirrors
HE	It's too late. The music ended.

IT'S ALL ABOUT

Touch...
Wanting
Your touch

To ignite mine

It's all about
Love...
Wanting
Your love
To marry mine

WE SHOULD BE DANCING

Hold me till
It hurts to stop and
Show me that your
Leg is strong enough
For two

Hold me till I smile
And nod to you and me
And back again till you
Show me that your
Arm is firm enough
For two

Grab my hand with yours
Till I swivel with pride
Side to side and back
Again legs open for you
Feeling the firmness
Of two

It happens so quickly
That time doesn't have
Time to stop, only later
In the folds of a dip
You show me the strength
Of two

And I know we should be dancing

CONNECTING

Connect the dots
It's a game you know
You against me
To score the most
But scoring isn't
Connecting

Connect the dots
It's a game, you know
Your life against mine
Your step against mine
Where do we begin
Connecting

Connect the dots
It's a game, you know
I'll box you out
Unless you box me first
Doing the box step and not
Connecting

Connect the dots
It's a game, you know
So stop it
Before it stops you
Stops you from
Connecting

Before the Dance ends

TAKING THE LEAD

He sat across from me
And I could feel the heat
As he spoke about the
Passion of the Dance.

It was in his voice and the
Way he bent forward and
Looked at me from the
Depth of his eyes where

Color met feeling and touched
My core when he told me
It doesn't happen often
Only when she gives herself

Fully and completely lets me
Lead. Not a control thing just
Two of us hearing the music
With our souls on Latin fire.

I couldn't wait for the lunch
To end so I could stand next
To him and breathe into his
Collar and reach out even

Though there was no music
And touch the warmth of His body
and feel the tone
Of his skin and know I had

Found the one to place me
In the right position where
I would stay and follow and
Not be afraid to give in.

MOONBEAN LOVE

The chemistry happened!
Not water and oil floating
Separately but matchbox
Sparks waiting to ignite.

Your touch caused shivers
Your look watered my eyes
With a rush of intensity
As I dipped into your soul

And saw there a like spirit
Reeking love, oozing love
Wanting to love me as I
Loved and wanted you.

We planned the night on
The beach wearing white
To match the moon casting
A gentle ray as you covered

Me with your body and the
Warmth of the flame launched
A togetherness we held onto
Breathlessly till morning

GOING SOLO

I practiced alone tonight, solo.
It took me longer to come
To a full stop, not feeling the
Strength of your leading me
To the perfect spot as we
Land together on the other
Side of the moon walking there
Among the leafless trees and
Caverns of sand while making
Our way cautiously to the top
As we go on living and longing
To smother each other completely

SECRET LOVER

I sighed and placed my head in the cradle
Tension filled every nook of my being
More to relieve than even I was able
More to do than usual it would seem

The dim-lit room was filled with restful sound
His hands broke through with warm, creamy softness
Touching deep spots that cried when they were found
Knowing after all the hurt would be less

Like dough he moved me front and back and over
Covers draped to hide what can't be seen
But in between those sheets he would discover
More of life, perhaps a lover in a dream

I moved the dough front and back and over
Tasty treats to tempt my secret lover

AMERICAN TRAVELER

I had three glasses tonight
One red and two white
Now I am missing you
And blue

POWER OF
THE DANCE
(2013)

It is time to come clean. It is time to touch and be touched. Touch me now.

—Alessandra

I AM A SEEKER

Of love
Of loving, learning, connecting

Of truth, not always
That's too serious

Of fun, most times
But kind of serious

Of love
Of loving, learning, connecting

Of answers
To questions causing pain

Of dreams
To help me live a life

Of love
Of loving, learning, connecting

Of challenges
Of friendships
Of oceans

Of love
Of growing, knowing, believing

Of love

HE DID IT AGAIN

He did it again, left me hot and
Bothered and didn't even suspect
That he had such power to bring
Me to my knees craving the
Sweetness of him satisfying

My lust, feeding the need that
Rises and falls somewhat like
The tide on a windy day with
Whitecaps swooning ashore but
With energy rising from below
High enough so the judges can
See it, deep enough so there is
Meaning and bold enough to
Show the character of the dance
Clearly and yet softly as it unfolds
Beat by beat on its way to submission

ACCENT

Go slow to be fast
Soft and hard
At the same time...

I don't get it
How can it be?

But then he showed me where to hold
So it would happen like that
Seamlessly as we stepped and
Paused pressing deep into each
Other—and I followed him

AND WE CONTINUED

He held my hips down firmly
And asked me to move my ribs
"Go ahead" ever so gently and
I let him show me the way
Side to Side catching his rhythm
But when he asked me to do it
On my own, I resisted, sensuously
Moving toward him just enough to
Let him know I had been captured...

IT HAPPENED TODAY

He reached it today as he reached for me
With warmth and strength that begged
For connection and made it seem so
Easy that I came to his side and stayed

He reached it today, the center of my soul
He got to the essence. He read in a minute
What I had been searching for, longing for
Craving, yes, needing to make me complete

His blue eyes looked into mine and he asked
Me to hold firmly. Forget the steps. Forget
What comes next or what passed. "Be in the
Present with me and I will take you there."

And I wanted to go there with him, to the
Place where the music rules and the dance
Floor disappears and the two of us feel the
Beauty and power and oneness of togetherness

It happened today. And I cried tears of joy.

ON THE WAY TO MYSELF

On the way to myself
I found you on the
Dance Floor with me

It was a special time
Since I felt your
Warmth and kindness
In the touch of your
Hand, the sound of
Your breath and the

Joy and Love you bring
To the Dance. The joy
And love you bring to me
The joy and love you
Share with life as you
Create wonder from the
Depths of your mind, the
Depths of your soul. You
Light the path on my way

And make it a way of expression
A safe harbor where dreams begin
And the boundaries of the floor
Reach beyond the sky. I take
Your hand to get there but
You allow me to find myself.

Thank you

TODAY I GRADUATED

It happened in American Smooth
And felt natural even though
I blinked after I did it from an
Outward spin. He drew me close
Next to him, breasts teasing, and
Asked me to place my hand on his...
Chest!

I did it and lived as I softly placed it
On a shirt of white with gnawing
Feelings about what went on under
The shirt while I nodded in response
To the power of the hold, keeping
Our connection firm I wanted his...
Leg!

Today I graduated because touching him
Had been too difficult to execute on the
Outside, too difficult to leave the waves of
My brain and meet the undulating waves of
Passion waiting to be released in the closeness
Of two lovers moving to the electricity of their...
Bodies!

SHAPE ME

Oh, Yes, you know how to do it!
Shape me in such a way that each side
Tells a story as it rotates teasingly reflecting
The desire I have to be powerful and sexy
And firm and irresistible as I chase you in
A Rumba walk, you backwards to my thrust

I learn over and over again that I must stand
On my own… dance my dance in response to
Your lead but not relying on it. Oh what a
Change from playing the meek one, pretending
To wait on the sidelines, leaving the limelight
For you to catch and add to the trophies on the wall

Now I get it. The weakness is just for show under
The covers. You really want me strong and able.
Confident that I can play my part, playing with
Your skin, caressing your cheek, pushing off from
Your chest. Yet in truth I want to cling to each part and
Lick and taste and thrive on the fluid of life you share

THEY BOWED

The dress hung empty on a hanger
Waiting to be filled

She wandered over gingerly
Touching the aqua satin and
Embracing the beaded bodice
Her eyes closed briefly
Imagining a Prince Charming
A Cinderella Waltz
Draped folds that come alive

Alive like she has since dancing
Alive like she is after three surgeries
Alive and dancing again and ready
To fill the dress

She dared to try it on

Closing the door of the dressing room
Letting a kind soul zip the zipper
Allowing a brief smile
When she knew it fit

Adjusting the shoulders
Walking to the room of mirrors
Giving a brief twirl
Then asking for his hand

He played the waltz
Then played with her
As she spun more bravely

The folds came alive
The dress filled with hope
An expression masked her face

With a glow that reached heaven

I wiped many tears from my eyes

They bowed

TOGETHER

You've got to be fast to be slow.
"Give me time," he pleaded
"To accent the step."

All I could think about was
His pressure beside me
Filling the space yet leaving
Enough room for a twist
Of the count that comes
At just the right time—together.

AFTER GRADUATION

I thought I graduated when I touched his chest
But today he asked me to grab his legs and then 'do
    the girly thing'
Back to front in the warmest of positions when
    close isn't close enough
Moving hips back and forth, sexy attitude and
    complete control.

Now how could control happen when his legs are
    harder than
Bricks and just standing there I wanted to caress
    them to
Mush and jump in and play Hide and Seek hoping
    he would
Find me first and play the man's role grabbing me
    with those
Legs of brick and show me it all meant more than a
    dance step.

Eventually I had to breathe and move on to the next
    step but it
Didn't get any easier because I had to keep the
    characteristic of
The Samba and still had a minute left to hold onto
    the rise of the steps
And roll of the hips and I wanted nothing more
    than to come to a stop

LEARN ME

You can read me on a page
Of words not written and
Each time I am surprised
When you ask me so coyly
"Are you excited?" "Are
You nervous?" "Are you
hungry?" How are you
So tuned into knowing?
How can you read me?
Why do you want to?

And, yet, when I have
Time to digest the questions
I smile inside and know
You are trying to learn
Me. Learn me so we can
Be better partners. Learn

Me so I can trust and be
Trusted. Learn me so
We can love. Learn me.

I'LL LEAD YOU INTO IT

Don't worry, I'll lead you into it softly
And he started to dance the step touching
Me this time gently as he guided me past
Him into the lushness of a forest surrounded
By leaves of green amidst a maze of trunks
Grounded and giving hints of the depth of
Their roots. It was damp and a bit chilly so
He wrapped me in his arms and led me
Towards the light shining in the distance
Promising the hope of a new beginning
Where the mistakes of the past would be
Erased and we would head confidently in
A line of dance created by our own music.

LETTING GO

There's a need to feel the dance through
The thighs and through the touch
Through the skin and through the
Tears that come after a practice
Because practicing is not real and
When it comes to real I have to let go

There's a need to feel free yet the need
To hold on is greater and yet it must be
Released to make the dance real and the
Connection move the audience to a climax
As well as the dancers and only truth can
Get the job done breathlessly if I let go

Where can I turn to make it happen? Is the
Answer on the Dance Floor or in the Practice
Room? Will it only come when feet ache and
Muscles burn with an intensity that can't be
Ignored even though the pain is less than
The birthing of my true self in order to let go

Please help me let go. Please help me split
The bars keeping me safe and protected. You've
Had a glance of the inside through the light of your
Electricity. I promise you there's more that will rise
In a Bolero, scrape your skin in a Rumba, resist to hurt
In a Tango and love you to pieces when I let go

Let me show you.

MY BODY IS REAL

Let me onto the dance floor to dance my dance
Knowing now that the secret is in the hands
Telling their story of want and desire to
Touch you in places that dare me to touch

And show you I care more than you know
And want you holding me close and closer
So I finally learn that my body is real
And can give joy and pleasure and love

Take me out of myself from a place deep
As the darkest cave holding a story of
Desire, never letting you know I had been
Taken, bought and belittled, but never sold

POWER OF THE DANCE

Feeling the power growing
Together and knowing
What can be said and what can
Be felt and how good it feels
And where it can be felt and
How to admit you feel
And how to let him know
You want to feel it and grab
On and hold the feeling till
You cry out asking for more

OUT OF CONTROL

I am getting better even though at times the
Feeling of heaviness sneaks in and ruins
What might otherwise be a perfect poise

It overwhelms me with sadness because
He is in love with the music and his
Dream of dancing in a wonderland

I want so much to make his fantasy real
And become part of it...my fantasy and
His beating out of control to a quickstep

MY DANCE PARTNER

You see his dancing body
And hips that move in Latin
From here to eternity

You see his strong frame
And sway that covers the floor
Skating to a waltz

What you don't see is
The beauty of a soul that
Offers strength and caring

A hand that leads quietly yet carefully
Firmly and knowingly, wonderfully
And always in the right direction

LET'S PLAY

Play with me today. I feel like it.
Go slower and stay longer. With
Your hand grasping mine gently
Yet sending its electric message
To lead the way causing me to
Feel feelings that won't be
Quieted by the beat of the music
Only by the beat of your skin.

IT ALL CAME EASY

The pressure's on to be hot and steamy
And honestly prove that blondes have more
Fun and I really don't have to work that hard
To make it happen because he touched me
And we loved in a way groping and smiling
And feeling and sensing a warmth that can't
Be faked, showing itself in motions of lust
And looks of trust and glances of wonder
And words of sex and thoughts of movement
And nods of approval and hopes of gaining
What we desired to feel complete and whole
Because we connected and chose to be one
Leaving differences behind and looking ahead
To dance in each other's arms, safe and loved.

EYES OF TIME

In eyes that are deep
And blue as the sea
He carries a message
Of the ages
Grounded in the now
But reaching back
As far as one goes
He tells a tale
Of caring, kindness
And understanding

We learn so much
From this soul that
Shares a time
When wonder kept
A heart beating gladly
He yearns so to
Grab us in its majesty

Some fear the feelings
Some grasp it
Some never will
But he tries with all
His might to hold
On and tell us
Love is dear

Look in those eyes
Dare it

TOUCH ME WITH YOUR SOUL

Touch me with your soul
And I will know who you are
As you light the universe
With your smile of relief
Not having to pretend, not
Having to be more or less
Than, not having to choose
Just having to be that
Which makes you whole to
Yourself and to me. Please
Touch me with your soul
So we can be one

OPENING THE DOOR

He's opening the door to more than I
Imagined and I'm finding there's more
Than the door that's opening. I'm ready to
Touch deeper, longer and firmer. To taste
It all. To give in more willingly and not feel
I have to stop before I really want to. I can go
Further on the way to saying "yes" to his lead
Without seeking approval or heeding a warning

Now I can look at his movement and
Respond to what I am missing down to the
Skin and the nakedness and the pressure
Knowing it's worth the fantasy since
Nine hours later I'm still panting

KALEIDOSCOPE

We shine from light reflecting and light emanating.
On any given day the light can be shaded by doubt
or glow with hope. Turn the pages slowly to catch
the patterns taking shape.

SHADES OF GREY
   ...when darkness blocks out the light

DAWN
   ...brightness peeking over the horizon

LIGHT OF DAY
   ...the power of color

SHADES OF GREY
   ...when darkness blocks out the light

Before I wore black and white and
Blended shades of grey avoiding real
Color and shape, turning just enough
To keep the truth hidden behind the crystals

Slowly the kaleidoscope rotated letting
In some light, light peeking into my soul.
I shuddered, frightened at what I would
Find but the crystals kept moving

Now light releases an intensity of desire
And determination to waltz onto the
Dance Floor of Life with brilliance
And feeling for the power of color

DAWN
...when darkness blocks out the light

I see it, the reflection in my eyes
For now I can spot a turn and look
At the light shining its response to
Me telling me it's safe to turn, safe
To see what's on the other side
The other side of me, the inside
Of me. It's peeking through and
I'm liking it. Liking the play, liking
The tease, Liking the thought that
I might really be real. And...
Liking it

LIGHT OF DAY
...the power of color

Colors burst through in orgasmic
Delight at the prospects of a new day.
Their energy fuels the Dance

AND NOW, GOOD-BYE

They sat at a table
Dinner over
Tears streaming loneliness

A new country
New beginning
Too far for her

No family
No language
Just dance

They sat at a table
Food not enough
To feed the soul

She reached for him
In her loneliness
Outstretched hand

Seeking the only
Answer in a touch
His touch

WILL YOU DANCE WITH ME?

They sat at a table
Tears streaming loneliness
She left

PLEASURE OF
THE DANCE
(2015)

I. AWAKENING

…Take my hand / And we're halfway there
—*Stephen Sondheim, from* West Side Story

THE SOUND OF A PLACE

The place is silence
Silence that reaches eternity
While quieting the voices
It's dark and not scary
It's dark and warm and comforting
No confusion, no directions, nothing

It's what I hear when no one calls
Except the longing to be known
The longing to be more
That refuses to be silenced

The yearning cries to be fed
Like cravings cry for sugar
I run to the silence
To that place where water and warmth
Dress my soul

Be quiet if you find me there
Don't break the silence with your touch
And know that whispers make glass explode
The heart dies, ears hear no more, voices stop

THE CAVE

It took your breath away seeing her
Twist and turn and bend and squirm
Fitting in between rocks
Almost as tight as the ride
Through the birth canal
Almost as traumatic

But the other side was light not darkness
Or was the light really darkness
It took many minutes for the eyes to adjust
Minutes when time stood still
When coming alive seemed like dying
Dark, still and ominous

The last push set her free
To roam in an interior where bats swarmed
And water dripped and secrets were kept secret
Hidden and encased in a place where
Hiding them kept them safe even from her
Little did she know the force they held

But it was time to explore
She felt ready to learn the why of her existence
And she crawled cautiously
Searching meant looking, searching meant pain
The pain of truths allowing her to be
But it was time to move on
And so moving through the darkness was necessary

The path was long and arduous
Inching forward carefully, holding onto rocks
Slick and cold, surfaces that trembled under her weight
She gained a foothold on a ledge and glimpsed a spark of light
That made her hope and feel the power of a new beginning
Yes, it was time the darkness fell away and let the future happen.

ALONE

Alone in a cave so dark
The start of eternity reverberated
I was finally able to hear your cry
The search was not easy

Years spent chasing the gnawing monster
Years spent hiding the shame
I got pretty good at it, too
Dancing along to everyone's beat

They'll never know I came from nothing
Raised by fear and longing
Untouched and abandoned
Shuddering in the silence of the night

Many times you asked me to come
I tried to get a glimpse through the crack
But it was always around the corner
Melted away before I could see or feel

And longing so to join the others
Yet longing so to be the only one
To stay on the hidden path, protected
To keep running on the path to nothingness

You wouldn't let me, kept eating away
Bit by bit you lured me on to awareness
Black isn't bad, it's a beginning
And white is covered in red for everyone

The cry is of another, of many others
Reach out and listen to their plea
Break the silence of the ages
Share your journey, let the soul live

DIG

Deeper Deeper
Maybe to China
Or perhaps
Out of this world
Out of myself
Break the crust
Crack the egg

What shape will I take
Not this one
Put together with Krazy Glue
Skin, bones, cells
Whose job it is
To keep me breathing
But who is me
Or who am I

Dig Dig
Take the time
Ask me
I might even tell

AT THE HEART OF IT

You'd think that after years
The shell would harden
Grow tough, stop needing to
Protect us from the onslaught

But we're not made that way
Time doesn't harden
Not like butterscotch topping
On soft serve ice cream

The space inside needs to be filled
Filled with love and acceptance
Filled with joy and caring
Filled with friendship that says, I count

And, I do

LOOK IN THE MIRROR

Look in the mirror
It tells the story of your choosing
You can see what you want
You can feel the difference
Causing happiness or longing
To be more than, less than, different

Look in the mirror
You can get to the real
Or cover it up with fantasy
Make the real you want
By adding sparkle or a feather

Look in the mirror
Transform till you become
True to the image
Be brave, trust, create
More than you expect

Dare to look

AWAKENING

I am the spirit you handle so gently
Allowing me to look in places left for dead
Allowing me to respond to your touch
And reach for the light hidden within

Yes, it is so frightening I resist as habit
Resists touching a hot stove or red coals
I resist being vulnerable and exposed
Pretending to be strong feels safer

But I know the time has come to
Open the door and look inside for
The truth. The joy we share gives
Me the courage to let it happen.

Hold me close.

II. DANCING AT SUNRISE

DANCING AT SUNRISE

I'm taking you to a place beyond our reality. You become the dance in this heavenly state, moving fluidly, hardly able to catch your breath as the song ends.

It's hidden so deep inside, that the
Prospect of finding it is frightening.
Yet the challenge of getting there
Promises more than space travel.

I am asked to let go and trust.
No need for a seat belt, no restrictions.

I want to trust but I'm overwhelmed
By not knowing, or by the thought that
I can never know, or by the thought

That once I take your hand and travel
There, there's no hope of return.

The silence will draw me in bit by bit.
Its very existence more powerful than
Trying or fighting or resisting.
I'll want to bottle it and have it again

And again, with you as my guide.
Take me to silence. Show me the way.

THE FIRST STEP

Take the first step into the unknown
Take it with me and trust that
You will know what to do
Without thinking, just feeling

Take the first step into the unknown
And we will become the music
Together as it's meant to be
No hesitancy, a total letting go

I'm willing to guide you gently and
Help you find answers in the expanse
And quiet of a universe that is waiting
To offer more than we can imagine

Take the first step

ON THE WAY TO MYSELF

On the way to myself
I found myself on the
Dance Floor with you.
It was a special time
Since I felt your
Warmth and kindness
In the touch of your
Hand, the sound of
Your breath and the

Joy and Love you bring
To the Dance. The joy
And love you bring to me.
The joy and love you
Share with life as you
Create wonder from the
Depths of your mind, the
Depths of your soul. You
Light the path on my way

And make it a way of expression
A safe harbor where dreams begin
And the boundaries of the floor
Reach beyond the sky. I take
Your hand to get there but
You allow me to find myself.

COVER ME

I'm shuddering not so you can see it
But I can feel it, shuddering ready to
Give birth to me. The universe is
Ready. I am ready but so afraid I
Am shuddering. Cover me with the
Cloak of your kindness. Warm me
With a gentle touch. Whisper softly
"I love you." Care more than ever.

QUIET

One must find the quiet of being in order to become.

I come to it every night
And find comfort in the quiet
It brings and the chance I have
To feel the energy in my
Fingertips roll forth feelings
Too raw to expose during the
Comings and goings of my day

I breathe deeply, sometimes
Close my eyes and hear the
Ring of the words as they
Capture an emotion be it
Love or lust or hope or fear
Or longing or desire

It's after the sound of the phone
Stops. It's after all the must dos
Have gone to sleep. It's when my
Stuffed animals talk to me without
Judging. It's when I'm not afraid
To reach for passion and find it

III. IAMI

ON EAGLE'S WINGS

We danced that day on eagle's wings
Carried in the grace of flight across
A dance floor that greeted us with
Kindness and love receptive to
Our every move. We danced that day
Connected. You knew it could happen.
I had to learn to trust, let go and
Soar. I pray to recreate this dream
Over and over again, breathing in its
Magnificence, living its complete joy.

THE CHIFFON ZONE

I live for it, for your touch.
I live for it, sensing the
Wonder of the folds of
Material draping softly
Down your side and gliding
To places I can only think
About as the lushness of
Chiffon makes itself felt
Against your skin
I want to tease you with
The silkiness of the material.
Guide me into your frame
And we will bathe in the
Flow of its endless rhythm

IN THE NOW

I'm ready to stop the noise.
I want us to happen.

To take the journey, I must be silent
I must quiet the chatter, clear the mind
Be a space blank enough for creation
Become the music, be still, be ready
Be ready to take your hand
Be ready to become us, not you and me
Not thought, not history, just movement
In the NOW in the universe of space

TO A NEW WORLD

We dance in a room circled by mirrors
And often I glance at the togetherness
Of our legs and find the image quite...
Quite! Quite what dancing is all about
And it's what keeps me coming back
Over and over again to imagine all
It could be or is or tries to be

And then today after a hard session
We ended up right at one of the mirrors
And he took my hand and we walked
Through it side by side to the new world
We create each and every time our bodies
Touch and bend and dip and connect
Becoming one with the music

There's not much air on the other side
So breathing deep is a must but
We've already practiced that and
Have it down to a science matched
By the rhythm of our rise and fall
And quite magically I'm light and
Airy and he is able to be magnificent

ENERGY / MATTER / SPEED / LIGHT

Simple words that bring Einstein to mind
Yet to grasp the words takes us beyond
Mind to the realm of thought where creation
Happens allowing millions of possibilities
Where speed doesn't matter but a spark of
Energy is needed to light the way and
Courage is needed to let the journey happen

I STAYED HOME TODAY

I stayed home today and faced quiet
And even though there were many
Times I felt the urge to run, I stopped.

I stayed home today and was born
Into the quiet of myself. Actually
It felt good. Actually it felt different.

There's a peek of excitement waiting to
Bloom yet I'm holding it back cautiously
As I let birth happen with my breath.

ANYTHING GOES?

I leave each day in ecstasy
Not believing it can get better
And yet it does and I try not
To wobble down the stairs
And yet I do from the pure joy
I have felt bending and twisting
And holding a vertical and holding
Myself together because I want to
Rush in giving it all at once but
I am learning to breathe and be
Strong and Quiet and Ready to
Take his hand and Dance to the
Lead he gives me where time and
Space defy reality. Where fantasy
Happens to "Anything Goes" and
It does.

IT'S NOW FOREVER

It's now or never or ever or someday
Or today or yesterday or tomorrow
It's all about time every day rushing
To catch it or make it or ignore it
But all I want to do is hold it so
Tenderly and sweetly and lovingly
And cherish every moment we have
Of it, being together and feeling the
Breath of it and knowing it will pass
Yet knowing the power of now

MIND TRAVEL

Come with me on a special journey
Through the looking glass of life.
Dare to open the door and withstand
The glare of a thousand suns with rays
Of light beckoning you to accept the
Invitation to greatness. Release the fear.
Take the first step and the next. Time
Is dear. Grab it and be strong. Follow
The quiet of a new tomorrow. A clean
Slate waiting for your brilliance. Dare.

BACK BEND

It looks like a back bend
But seeing is really not
Believing because what
You see is only an illusion
Yet not the same for what
You feel from the heat of
A connection that is really
On its way to taking a position
That keeps you looking for an
Answer: Is It All Really Possible?

A SILENT BEYOND

I could have been quiet today but
It was just too difficult and many
Times I just wandered around trying
To find my place, any place that
Would allow me to breathe deeply
And calm the beat I was feeling even
Though I wasn't dancing. Like a drug
The urge to partake overcame any sense
Of order or direction or belief that I
Could do it on my own. What fun is
That, making it happen without you?
So I tried the sweet thing and ten of
Them didn't do it either so I took to
Writing and losing myself in the words
Which have a special birthplace around
The throat chakra even though they come
Out silently they leave me calm. But I do
need you to take me to silence with your
Gentle touch and soft body leading me
In the direction I am craving out there
In a silent beyond where temptation
Inspires. So please come back!

ON TRUST....

Do I trust you with my spirit or my steps
Or is that the same thing when you
Offer me your hand and ask me to follow?
Do I trust you with my will or my voice
Or the balance of power that lies in between
As our bodies search for connection?

Trust powers our journey to togetherness
Trust allows my shape to be shaped
Don't let me melt. Shape me!

IAMI

It's after midnight when I calm down enough to tell you clearly
Why I dance, why I dance to write, why I write to dance
So why does it always sound so confusing when the steps
Are clear, clear to me, one two three going to eight
Not many numbers to confuse, eight at the most but they
Do a job on my brain... a job that had to be done, a job
I begged them to do... That's why it happened

I was blocked, locked, stuck. Darn stuck like the thickest of
Mud. Black dirty mud. Sucking me into a nothingness of
Yeses and pleasing and going through the motions with
No life of its own and no life of my own. I was suffocating.
Slowly yet surely... life draining out of me in being right.

You dug into the mud. Got your hands dirty in the thick of it
Creating space that would allow me to create myself in
A new vision, no, not a new vision, a true vision. Space
That would let me be me. The dance demanded it. The music
Allowed it. You gave me the nudge... just enough to
Start the words flowing in rhyme and sometimes not in rhyme but
In time to save me. Listen to the words of passion, the words of
Power and follow their progress to a pleasure that will give you the
Courage to unlock. Don't be afraid. I'll take your hand.

HERE I AM

The time will come when the
Need to blossom is so powerful
That bursting forth in
Atomic shape is the only option

★

I'm there now on the launch pad
Only deep breaths and faith are
Packed for my journey

★

It happens in the space between breaths
Where life comes alive and takes shape
Giving me time to embrace the gifts and
Create a being of my own from the power

★

 A different being from the first
A step beyond the second
Determined to find the light
Of the outermost stars in
Every step we take together

★

Touch me

WHAT DOES IT MATTER?

What does it matter that rooms move
And spaces change because you
Invite me with the same grace and
Style showing me you care deeply
And encouraging me to come to you
Softly and gently yet firmly with poise

What does it matter that I can sense
Your touch so firmly and strongly
Yet lightly and confidently with
Just enough power that it does matter
Because that touch tells me how and
Where and how much and I know why

PERMISSION

They're starting to peak through
Moments of stillness during
A day of the usual madness
Brought on by becoming true
To myself and letting it feel good
Because feeling good is okay
Yes, it's okay to feel good
It's okay to take a deep breath
Like the one I just took getting
Ready to know why I finally
Let myself be okay and finding
The place where I can make it
Happen over and over again.
It feels different. Grounded,
Special, rich, satisfied, happy
Thank you for giving me
Permission

YES, IT DOES MATTER

That every time I reach for your hand
You cover mine gently reminding me

To be ready and wait
To be there in the now
To know it will come

And yet, I find it so hard
To wait, to be in the now
To come as gently as you
Want me to into your

Arms, breathing your
Breath, waiting and knowing
It does matter

TANGO POWER

The room was warm, the connection steamy
The Gotan beat relentless as I turned
Inward to quiet the pull of excitement that
Could ruin the power of the moment that
Would grow into moments if I let it happen
And I did, watching hours tick by and
Barely finding the breath to continue
Around the room and around your body as
You urged "Into me!" And I followed
The lead where I wanted to be more than
Anything while playing with the distance
Between us as we danced the dance
Capturing their souls with our energy

IV. DANCING BEYOND EINSTEIN

and as Einstein said: There are two choices on how to view the world:
Nothing is a miracle, or everything is a miracle.

AND IT IS A MIRACLE

It is a miracle to move through space
It is a miracle to move through space with musicality
It is a miracle to share the movement through space with another
It is a miracle to hear the sound of the music and capture its essence as one

TO DANCE WITH EINSTEIN

Will the usual face paint and upsweep
Meet his expectations and be dynamic
Enough to take me out of this world
To meet him on the dance floor of
The Galaxy?

Will weightlessness make it easy to
Follow all that this mind of mine can
Conceive or will a dome offering a
Gravity I know be part of his grand
Design?

I'm ready now to join him where matter
Doesn't matter and where the speed of
Light will give us the energy for a
Connection that is more powerful than
Fusion.

Oh how I long to dance this dance among
The stars and feel the warmth of his
Closeness urging us to catch the pulse
Of a time beyond now

MAKING SENSE

We come together each day to make sense of a cosmos
Unlike the scientists who are trying to make sense of
A world with rules and use of superior intellectual power
We search for meaning and answers in the grace of movement
Using tools human in nature and godlike in form and substance

Some look for absolute truths measured by tools of metal
Others measure truth in response to touch and breath
Some seek satisfaction owning their ideas materially
Others gain enlightenment from the energy of connection
Each one desires to escape the mundane of their personal experience

I'll choose your world of music and speed and light
Let me feel the texture of the sound reverberate in my veins
For hours after the steps have caused me to gasp for air
The vastness of the universe asking me to let go and follow
And find in the power of flight the answers I seek

IT'LL COME

It'll come if I'm quiet
It'll come if I'm patient
It'll come if I surrender
It'll come with purity

A lot to ask? Yes, a lot
But the journey to quiet
Has begun already
Different? Oh, yes
Difficult? Oh, yes

And I'm looking for
A road sign that says
Patience. And another
One advising surrender

How strange to lump them
With purity... clean and white
Stark and unfeeling.
Wouldn't it be better to
Look for confidence

With it, I can be quiet and
Patient. With it, I can
Surrender. But with it
I can show the real stuff
As I reach higher than high
Yet still find myself in your arms

GIRL IN THE BACKWARDS SKIRT

Today a person appeared on the dance floor
In a long black backwards skirt, quite amusing
She looked like she might have a glimmer of
An idea about what to do, but the how-to was
Missing and the direction of her gaze questionable

Perhaps she needed a good look in the mirror to
Set her straight and allow her to come out in
Her own clothes toward her partner and even with him
That would have been an easier picture to watch
Instead of the backpack trailing behind her backwards skirt

Let's tell her it's okay to drop the baggage and rise one
Step at a time free and clear of the past seeking a now
That opens doors to the self and allows her to be free
Let's tell her it's okay to meet him face to face and look
In his eyes of blue truthfully and purely showing bliss

Let's even tell her that the skirt was inside out and needs
To be righted as she steps out captivatingly in her real dress
Let's tell her it's okay to be herself and join her own couple.
Let's tell her to dance! Let's tell her it's okay.

SPEED

Answer me fully as you
Press your foot on the floor
And receive the message I send

Now don't tense up just take
The next lead as smoothly
Letting me encourage you
To move with my body

Yes, it's okay to mold but
Don't melt and don't rush
The feelings you'll feel if
You watch your speed and
Take it slowly, deeply and
Wisely, like I send it

CREATING SPACE IN THE HEART

I am purely truth springing forth from
A place I'll call soul for now or me or
Us growing strong as we experience
Blockages being removed and fires
Igniting from the depth of our hearts
As trust is kindled and nurtured
And serves to make us love-full and
Power-full and real standing erect
Being on one's own yet causing a
Field of magnetism that can be read
At a glance, felt from a distance and
Draws us fearlessly into a space that
Is protected by our courage to step out
Into the unknown bound together with joy

CREATION

He offered me his hand saying,
"Take the breath, your breath
The fuel to start our journey
On a beam of light into the
Vastness of the universe as
The lead I give you can be
Grasped with the softness of
Your spirit and follow the
Nothingness of time that we
Create as one, relative
To what matters to each of us"

DANCING CHEEK TO CHEEK

They captured the essence of Fred Astaire
And Ginger Rogers dancing cheek to cheek
In a performance that sent chills through
The audience and left onlookers open-mouthed

On the dance floor the past became the
Present as they swirled with a rise and fall
Not clinging to each other but dancing as
One while filling the room with electricity

It was the ultimate joining of music and dance
Touched by the memory of magnificent costuming.
I tried to find the secret of their motion, to steal it
As she responded effortlessly to his lead

They moved slowly, a micro bit of time to capture the beat
His strength matched the notes and brought them together
Making a connection, joining on shoulder and hand
Becoming one in spite of their differences

V. WHY WE DANCE

To watch us dance is to hear our hearts speak.

—*Hopi Indian Saying*

OLGA BOGDANOV

Dance gives me a feeling like none other. It is the endless opportunity to become better every step of the way—to enjoy the process as well as the performance. I cherish every moment of interaction with my peers and students. It is a wonderful profession.

About Olga Bogdanov: Olga is a former Competitive American Smooth and Standard Champion. She holds titles as a bronze medal winner at the European Championships in 1996 and Russian Open medalist and World Representative in 1998. In 2001, Olga and partner Sasha Bogdanov were Rising Star International Standard Champions. Currently she competes with her students in all levels of dance, coaches, performs, choreographs and judges. I meet with Olga regularly for coaching lessons and am amazed by her ability to articulate and transmit the expressiveness she brings to her performance. She willingly shares her "secrets" and thrives on the progress her students demonstrate. Olga is a true teacher.

MICHAEL CHAPMAN

Thanks to dancing, I have traveled over two million miles around the planet in a narrow, metal tube with wings! For over two decades, I have choreographed, taught, and organized dance productions, including nearly fifty competitions worldwide. The Millennium Dancesport Championships is my flagship event and it is the epitome of what I strive to achieve in everything I do: to realize my artistic vision with a creative flair that inspires everyone to dance and, also, to do it with a warmth and personal touch so that everyone feels welcome.

Just as dancing demands two bodies to synchronize in harmony, it takes a talented and dedicated team working cohesively: supporting and connecting with each other to produce a positive and magical experience.

Every dancer whom I have known has a reason and purpose driving their passion. My congratulations to Janice Sussman for her tenacity and spirit, for expressing her artistic sensuality, and for capturing in words what dancing evokes in her soul. I hope this book uplifts every dancer to find their personal inspiration and have the courage to let it lead the way.

About Michael Chapman: Michael has competed professionally and was the 1992 and 1994 World Open Exhibition Dance Champion in Holland, 1992 and 1995 U.S. Pro-Am Grand Champion, 1993 Triple Crown Exhibition Dance Champion, and Canadian and British Exhibition Champion. He has guest starred at the 1995 Super Bowl Half Time show and PPS Unforgettable Boleros special. He is an international adjudicator, coach, and choreographer. Michael has hosted tours all over the globe to discover the roots of The Dance. It is his love, his life.

PEN AND LISA COSBY

We dance because we can have fun doing it together! We experience a spiritual and physical connection and can share its beauty and excitement. We even teach new amateur partners and get such joy seeing their progress and love of the dance develop. It's a wonderful passion.

About Pen and Lisa Cosby: Pen and Lisa are a husband and wife team, dancing as partners in the Amateur Division.

LARRY DEAN

In keeping with his warm style and professional presence, Larry Dean joined our table for breakfast during one of his magnificent competitions in Aventura, Florida. He took the time, as always, to share his insight into why we dance.

Larry has been organizing competitions for forty-four years and began this journey with a single-day event at a Knights of Columbus Hall in West Palm Beach. He has owned three ballroom dance studios and created the Crown Jewel and Triple Crown Dancesport Championships with his wife, Diane. These events are the first and longest-running Dancesport Series in America. Giving the customer the best experience was his goal and he will always be remembered for hosting magnificent international events at the Breakers Hotel in Palm Beach.

But how did he start to dance? Yes, it was a girl he met while working on submarines. She gave him a guest pass to an Arthur Murray Studio and his funniest memory is believing that when they called him "Twinkle Toes Larry," he would have to actually get up on his toes and dance.

Larry was not new to music. He had played the drums, so keeping the beat was easy. He was brought up with Gospel, Blue Grass, and Country music. In fact, Larry's father was a singer who sang in church with Dolly Parton.

To Larry, dancing is a perfect combination of his love of people and love of music. It is food for his soul. "We dance," says Larry, "for Pure Enjoyment." And the twinkle in his lovely blue eyes is proof.

About Larry Dean: Larry is a national dance adjudicator, coach, and examiner. He is past president of Florida Dance Teachers Association and past president of National Dance Teachers of America.

PAOLO AND LIENE DI LORENZO

Paolo: Dancing lets me express without words how I feel every day of my life—be it happy, sad, excited, devastated. The freedom of the form gives me freedom of expression with no holding back.

Liene: Dancing is a very important part of me as a human being. I've been dancing forever. Dancing describes me. It is who I am.

About Paolo and Liene Di Lorenzo: This championship partnership has been a force since 2004. With U.S. National Professional Classic Show Dance title and finalist positions at the World Professional Classic Show Dance Championship, they bring you to the peak of excitement and emotion with their spectacular performances. For them, dancing is a conversation that allows them to achieve perfect communication. This is the beauty of the dance at its core.

OLGA FORAPONOVA

We dance because it is part of our life! It is so powerful to feel the control we have of our bodies as we become the music. It is exquisite to join with a partner and perform. I cherish every memory I have of becoming part of the world of dance.

About Olga Foraponova: Olga is a two-time U.S. National Ballroom Champion and World Showdance Finalist with partner David Hamilton. She has competed internationally and won competitions in Leningrad, Riga, and Cheliabinsk. Her dancing was showcased on national television in PBS's Championship Ballroom Dancing. *She travels throughout the United States judging, teaching, coaching, and lecturing professionals and amateur students. Olga adds a touch of class to your dancing because of the* brilliant combination of strict adherence to technique coupled with exquisite creative interpretation. It is an honor to work with her. Olga organizes the Autumn Dance Classic in San Francisco with Jonathan Wilkins and owns and operates the Dorothy Jayne Studio in Everett, Washington.

JULIA GORCHAKOVA

One of the most important reasons why I dance is because I love it. Dance has made me who I am today. It helped me develop character and find a great career, and has taught me how important determination is in becoming a skilled competitor. Through dance, I met the best husband in the world!

About Julia Gorchakova: Julia's Artistry in Motion Dance Dresses send dancers on the floor in the most elegant style. Julia and her team work tirelessly to insure the dress matches the dancer, not only in fit but in the impact that results when dancer and dress are in perfect harmony. She is the twelve-time U.S. Rhythm Champion and three-time World Mambo Champion.

CRAIG GORDON

Dance is a journey. Dance is living. I am just living the journey as the story unfolds. Connecting to myself, connecting to my partner, connecting to others is intoxicating, romantic, and so beautiful. It is summed up in a line from a Sanskrit text written 5,000 years ago that captures the essence: "The soul Dances in...Happiness."

About Craig Gordon: I thank Craig for sharing his expertise and love of dance as teacher, coach, and friend. We compete nationally and internationally in American Smooth and American Rhythm.

WENDY JOHNSON

Dancing has no boundaries . . . everyone can participate. Dancing is healthy, social, and fun.

About Wendy Johnson: A classically trained Ballet and Ballroom dancer, Wendy has won many prestigious competitions and has choreographed and coached such stars as Cheryl Burke, Nick and Lena Kosovich, Tony Dovolani and Elena Grinenko. A former New Zealand Ballroom and Latin Champion, she is co-organizer of Holiday Dance Classic in Las Vegas. She has judged competitions internationally and shares her professionalism and experience with the dance community through her dedication and commitment to excellence. She choreographs for Dancing with the Stars, *and dances because it's her favorite thing to do.*

KASIA KOZAK

With a dynamic glow in her eyes, and exuding a burst of energy, Kasia told me, "That's my way of meditating!" It's not the usual first response. However, we learn from this powerful coach that this is how she connects to herself and others through the feelings, emotions and spirit of Dance.

She continues, "It is where there is no right or wrong way to feel. Everyone's response is perfect and reflective of their interpretation of the music and movement. But," she says with authority, "in order for your audience to read your message, you must be clear and direct, in time with the music, and connected to your partner."

*About **Kasia Kozak:*** *Professional Latin Champion, Founder of Kasia's High Heels Boot Camp and Co-founder of Dance Like a Champion, Kasia is an accomplished coach, judge, and choreographer. Her spiritual being and boundless energy ignite the dance floor.*

PURPLE TIGER STYLISTS: MARGARET BURNS AND ELIZABETH CARTIER

Margaret: I can't imagine a world without dancing. It would be a horrendous place. I dance because it's in my blood! And, to dance we must use both sides of our brain. There's logic in the technique and an organization in how we move. And then the emotions kick in. It's perfection!

Elizabeth: I live for the love of dance and love of life. I love how it makes me feel. I love the beauty of the partnership. I dance for love.

*About **Purple Tiger:*** *Margaret Burns and Elizabeth Cartier unleash their special magic in hair and makeup design through their company, Purple Tiger. They specialize in fantasy looks that are crafted to match the dancer. Their hours range late into the night (midnight is not unusual) and start incredibly early (3:00 a.m. is sometimes possible). Margaret and Elizabeth are always ready and willing to be by the side of their dancers, and their quality service does make a difference. Their clients take on the saucy, sexy, and sophisticated look of a Purple Tiger creation. Margaret Burns is a World Exhibition Champion, a U.S. Ten Dance Champion, and a world class adjudicator. Elizabeth competes professionally with Sergey Bondarenko.*

DAVID ROSARIO AND OLGA BARASHIHINA

David: Why we dance? It's addicting. It's in my blood. And, I'm drawn in by the energy, by the people and by the opportunity I have to share my experience—not to mention my grandmother, Josefina Rosario, was a very famous Tango dancer. It's why retiring is really out of the question.

Olga: Dance is the hidden language of the soul. It represents true freedom of expression, which is priceless. As a partner dance it gives you the opportunity for the masculine and feminine sides of each dancer to meet in harmony and keep their energy in balance. The key is to find the right partner who can achieve this balance with you. It is a journey of learning and it is not only fun but offers an opportunity to develop other aspects of social life—communication and body language skills, learning to present yourself, and gaining confidence. Since I always knew I wanted to be a teacher and since I love working with people, coaching and teaching dance have given me this opportunity. To see the students learn and enjoy is very exciting for me. It gives me great pleasure to share my love of the Dance.

About David Rosario and Olga Barashihina: David Rosario is a nine-time U.S. title finalist, capturing three of these U.S. titles with his partner, Olga Barashihina. Together they placed fifth in Open to the World. David started dancing at age seventeen in Savannah, Georgia. Olga was born in Riga, Latvia, where she was Latin Champion. She represented Latvia in World and European Championships and placed ninth in the World Cup. American Smooth is their niche and five years after retiring, they continue to perform and coach.

SAM SODANO

I was a high school student when I started dancing. The year was 1960 and partner dancing was still in vogue. My father arranged for my partner, Gail Weise, and me to compete on the *Clay Cole* television show, an east coast smaller version of the popular *American Bandstand*. We won the live telecast, an event that set the course for the rest of my life.

Once I experienced that indescribable feeling of the music, the rhythm and a partner, I couldn't imagine any other career path. My desire to dance led me to an Arthur Murray studio and reached a high as a competitor at the prestigious Blackpool, England, event and other European and North American competitions as a judge and competition organizer.

I was lucky to find dance at a young age and to enjoy a successful career. As a competition organizer, I hope to provide fulfilling dance opportunities for people of all ages and all walks of life.

About Sam Sodano: It has been an honor for me to compete at Sam's events because they exude an air of professionalism and intensity that motivates dancers to put the effort and focus necessary to perform at their best. His Ohio Star Ball is a landmark competition and he has brought an energy to Galaxy Dance Festival which he organizes with Marianne Nicole, Linda Deane, and John DePalma in Phoenix, Arizona; the Atlanta Open organized with Debbie Avales and Sarwat Kaluby, and Holiday Classic presented in Las Vegas with Mary Murphy and Wendy Johnson. Sam was the recipient of the BBC & C Lifetime Achievement Award in 2014. Sam adds judging and coaching to his busy schedule but always has a minute to pass on a word of encouragement and a warm smile to dancers of all levels. Sam is truly a legend.

SHARON SAVOY

To answer the question why we dance is to ask why we need breath to live.

I was trained at the School of American Ballet, directed by George Balanchine whose famous quote describes my passion. "I don't want dancers who want to dance. I want dancers that need to dance."

My love of *pas de deux,* partnering, led me to the ballroom exhibition field where the addition of lifts provided an aerial dimension in which to express. Exhibition style dance combined the romance of dancing with a man with the exhilaration of soaring through the air and of floating suspended in the palm of my partner's hand. It isn't the winning trophies or standing ovations I recall; it is the sublime thrill of performing and leaving it all on the floor.

I have been fortunate to have had a long and successful career in dance and can't imagine my life without it. The following quote from the ballet movie *The Red Shoes* sums it up quite succinctly.

Boris Lermontov: Why do you want to dance?
Victoria Page: Why do you want to live?
Boris Lermontov: Well I don't know exactly why, but I must.
Victoria Page: That's my answer, too.

About Sharon Savoy: *Sharon Savoy is a ballroom phenomenon. She started her training at the illustrious School of American Ballet under the tutelage of the legendary George Balanchine. From there she found her true love, pas de deux, or the art of partnering, and became a decorated ballroom dance exhibition champion. Her biggest accomplishments include being a three-time World, four-time Blackpool, seven-time U.S. Open and three-time Star Search Dance Champion, being the featured dancer in the Hollywood movies* Dracula: Dead and Loving It! *and* Head of State, *as well as performing on* Regis and Kathie Lee, Entertainment Tonight, *PBS, Miss America, Sydney Olympics and at the Kennedy Center.*

BRAD STEIN

We sat at dinner together and I had an opportunity to share the spirit of a very special dancer. Why do we dance? We dance because we have to. Dance is in our blood and is a driving force that keeps us excited and exhilarated. We share with the audience a moment in time that is purposeful. Our intention is pure and puts us in harmony with the universe. Life is dance. Dance is life.

In an effort to reach for perfection, Brad warns that we must not lose sight of the beauty and richness of our performance. It is a life lesson to focus on the positive energy in all our endeavors and not get angry about the mistakes we make. In fact, according to Brad, the entire experience is about Positive Attention. It is about the Positive Attention we get from the audience and from our dance community. It is about the Positive Attention we give ourselves for the hard work and commitment that goes into our performance.

Brad's advice to every student: Listen to your partner by holding yourself correctly. And, as a final quote he said with amazing conviction: "Love is the answer regardless of the question."

About Brad Stein: *Brad Stein is a Theater Arts World Champion, a coach, judge, and pro-am competitor.*

WWW.TRILOGYOFDANCE.COM